that they did not know everything—and so they also had a shrine to 'THE UNKNOWN GOD'. Perhaps that way they were sure they had covered every option!

In our own society there is increasing fascination with spirituality, even among people who never attend a conventional church. Like the altars on the street corners in Athens, that fascination testifies to a deep hunger in the human heart. We know that life is more than we can see and feel; deep down, we know that we are more than animals. One great thinker, Augustine, expressed it like this: 'God has made us for himself, and our hearts are restless until they find rest in him.'

So, it may get us 'laughed out of college', but what if… what if the reason for the sense of God in our hearts is the simplest of them all—that God himself has put it there? What if it is true, as the Bible says, that God has **'set eternity in [our] hearts'?**[1] Follow me as we follow Paul's words together. They will help us understand the truth, and Jesus said, **'You will know the truth, and the truth will set you free.'**[2]

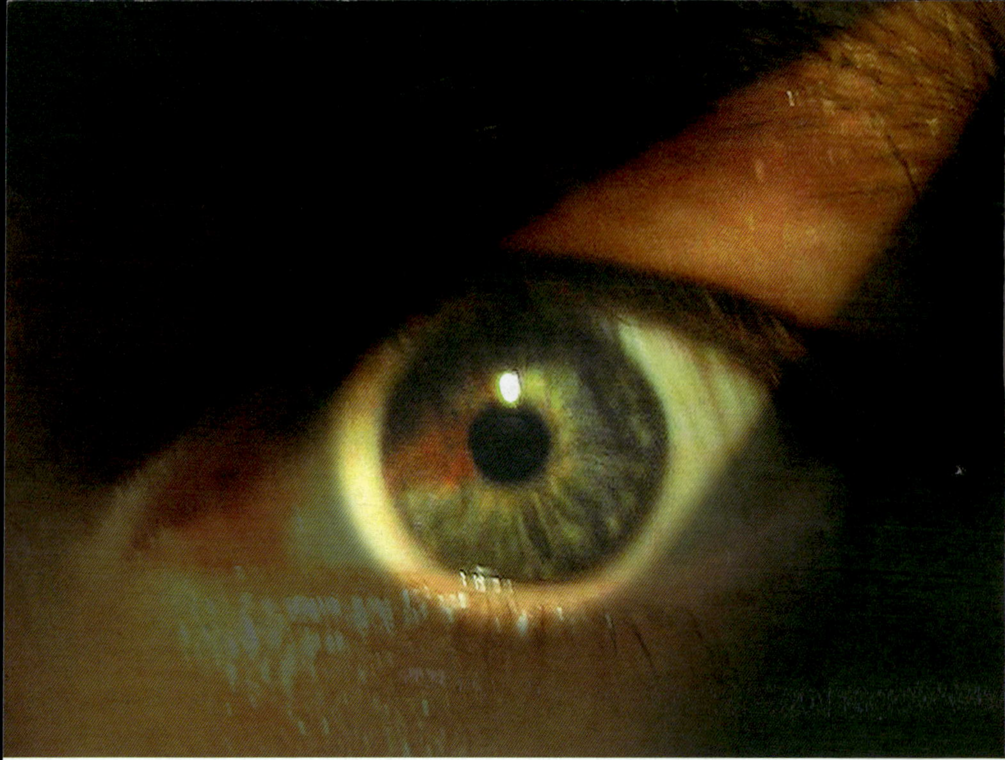

Is God near?

'an altar with this inscription:
TO AN UNKNOWN GOD' Acts 17:23

Before we go any further, we need to think a little bit about the man who spoke the words recorded in Acts 17.[3] He is the apostle Paul, sometimes called 'St. Paul'—a man God changed. The God of the Bible is not only very real, but he is also active in the world, changing the lives of men and women. Paul was one such man.

Paul had been brought up as a Jew, and belonged to the strictest sect of the Jews, the Pharisees. In those days he was known as Saul, and was a violent opponent of the Christian faith, persecuting Christians even to death. However, that all changed one day when he was on the road to

Damascus: a bright light shone from heaven and he heard the voice of Jesus speaking to him. (The story is recorded in Acts chapters 8 and 9.) From then on, he became a hard-working and very effective missionary, preaching the gospel throughout the known world. He was appointed an apostle by the Lord Jesus—that is, someone who spoke and wrote with God's authority. At least thirteen of the New Testament letters were written by him.

Athens had once been the centre of a great empire, but by Paul's day that empire had been replaced by the Roman Empire. Still, Athens was a very important city and it was regarded as a great centre of learning. Those who loved to debate—and had the time—still gathered there and spent their time **'doing nothing but talking about and listening to the latest ideas'** (Acts 17:21). But their religious ideas were so vague, and God seemed so distant, that they had erected an altar 'to an unknown God'.

Round about AD 50, Paul found himself in Athens, waiting for his companions to join him. As he wandered around, he noticed that the city was full of idols. Never one to resist a challenge, he began to debate in the market-place with those who were there. This led to an invitation to the Areopagus—a very prestigious court, already very ancient, that was probably responsible for licensing public lectures. To these people, Paul explained his message. Because he was an apostle, what he said had all the authority of God behind it, and it was therefore included in Scripture. Jesus said, **'Scripture cannot be broken.'**[4]

Can we know God?

'What you worship as something unknown I am going to proclaim to you ...' *Acts 17:23*

Imagine for a moment that you are led for the first time into a room—perhaps a study you have never been in before. As you look around, there are some things you recognize: you are very sure about the chair, for example, and you know what it is for. There are other things you know about—maybe a computer—but you may not know what the owner of the study uses it for. You could guess, and you might be right or wrong.

If you had closed your eyes as you were led in, you would be less sure about what was in the room; but you could feel around and, in between bumps and bruises, still get some idea of the furniture, and some small idea of what it might be used for. You might even be able to work out—or guess—some things about the person who uses the study. But it would be hard to be certain about anything.

Even if the human race *is* incurably religious, can we be certain of anything at all about God? After all, there are so many religions, and each of them thinks it has the truth. Have we just been left to wander and grope around in the dark?

Like the rest of us, he knew from Creation that there is a God: **'The heavens declare the glory of God.'**[5] The universe cannot 'just exist'—its design is so intricate that there has to be a Designer. (I will enlarge on this a little later on.) Yet if that were all Paul knew, he could not have helped the Greeks—or us.

But Paul was also a Jew, and for two thousand years God had been making himself known to the Jewish people. The Old Testament records that revelation; think of it as the owner of the study telling you, in the dark, what furniture is in the room and what it is for. And God's revelation had now reached its highest point in Jesus. When the angels announced Jesus' birth, they called him **'Christ the Lord'**,[6] and 'Lord' was the way the Jews referred to God. Unlike Moses—who centuries earlier had given God's law to the people—Jesus came full of grace and truth.[7] That is, he came not merely to tell the truth about God, but also to reveal God's grace—his kindness—to the world that did not deserve it. With Jesus, God continues to tell us what is in the study—but he has also switched on the light *and* introduced us to the study's owner, so that we may know the truth much more fully. Jesus said, **'I am the way, and the truth and the life. No one comes to the Father except through me.'**[8]

Where does the world come from?

'The God who made the world and everything in it…' Acts 17:24

Our universe is believed to be more than twenty thousand million light years across—that is, light travelling at 186,000 miles per second takes more than 20,000,000,000 years to cross the universe. In it there are perhaps one hundred thousand million galaxies, and maybe ten thousand million million million stars.[9] Where did it all come from? Why is there 'something' instead of 'nothing'? The Bible's answer is the one that Paul proclaims to the Greeks: God made it.

The universe did not always exist. **'In the beginning, God created the heavens and the earth.'**[10] We know when we see a watch keeping good time that the watch had a designer and a maker. God is the designer and maker of the universe.

That makes sense. The universe is obviously here, and there are only three possible explanations for that. One is that it has always been here—it is eternal. That seems unlikely, and many scientists—perhaps most—tell us that it is impossible. A second is that the universe created itself—which is obviously contradictory. For that to happen, the universe would have to exist before it existed! The only remaining possibility is that it was created by an infinite and eternal outside being—a being that has always existed and never had or needed a Creator. That being is what the Bible reveals to us as God.

God *was* always there—he is an eternal God. Eight times the Bible describes God as **'from everlasting'.**[11] In fact, he is **'from everlasting to everlasting'**[12]—without a beginning and without an end. All created things have a cause; but God is uncreated, and the cause of all that happens.

Most remarkably, the Bible insists, too, that the God who made the world is Jesus. He is the eternal God; Jesus himself claimed it. For example, Abraham was the ancestor of the Jews and lived two thousand years before Jesus was born, so Jesus must have been claiming to be eternal when he said, **'Before Abraham was born, I am.'**[13]

Even more clearly, the apostle John calls him 'the Word' and declares, **'the Word was God'**[14] and the apostle Paul speaks of Jesus as **'God over all, forever praised.'**[15]

Hasn't science disproved God?

'The God who made the world and everything in it…' Acts 17:24

Some years ago, a group of evolutionary scientists at a conference were asked by their speaker, 'Can you tell me anything you know about evolution, any one thing, any one thing that is true?' There was an embarrassed silence for a while, after which one scientist said, 'I do know one thing—it ought not to be taught in high school.'[16]

That story is important because many people who are not scientists assume that science is about certainty. It is not—it is about the pursuit of certainty. In fact, Karl Popper—the twentieth century's foremost philosopher of science—said that it is inevitable 'that every scientific statement must remain tentative for ever.'[17] So much for certainty!

On the other hand, we have to understand that there is a great deal of evidence—scientific evidence, if you want to call it that—that God exists. Late in life, the philosopher Anthony Flew, a professor at Oxford and lifelong atheist, finally admitted defeat. The evidence was clear: there is an intelligent designer (a God) behind the universe.

One strand of such evidence is the so-called 'fine tuning' of the universe—that is, infinitesimal variations in the strength of some of the 'laws of nature' would have made the universe, and life, impossible. For example, Stephen Hawking (perhaps the most famous scientist of our day) has commented on the relative masses of protons and electrons in atoms: 'The remarkable fact is that the values of these numbers seem to have been very finely adjusted to make possible the development of life,' he says.[18] But finely adjusted by whom—if not by God?

That may be one of the reasons why many, many scientists are convinced believers in God. Of course, that doesn't prove that there is a God or that the Bible is true. But it certainly proves that, if we think 'science has disproved God' or that 'modern science has already dissolved Christianity in a vat of nitric acid'[19] we are absolutely wrong. The facts are otherwise.

Does God need us?

'...he is not served by human hands...' Acts 17:25

The Greeks believed in many gods; Paul knew (because the Old Testament told him) that there was only one. The one true God is vastly different from the gods the Greeks were imagining, in at least three ways.

Firstly, the true God is **'Lord of heaven and earth.'**[20] Greek gods were limited—there was a god for the sea, a god for war, a different god for love and so on. But Paul's God is absolute Lord over all things. Anything that exists was made by him. Everything that exists is ruled by him. That includes me, and it includes you, too.

Secondly, the true God **'does not live in temples'**.[21] He cannot be restricted in that way: God is everywhere. **'Where can I go from your Spirit? Where can I flee from your presence? If I go up to the heavens, you are there; if I make my bed in the depths, you are there. If I rise on the wings of the dawn, if I settle on the far side of the sea, even there your hand will guide me, your right hand will hold me fast.'** [22] Wherever you are right now, God is with you, watching and knowing everything. As one person in the Old Testament said, **'You are the God who sees me.'**[23]

Thirdly, God does not need us. Though some religions believe their gods have to be fed or served in some way, Paul tells his hearers that the true God can never need anything from us. He is self-existent (nobody and nothing made him), and he is also completely self-sufficient (he needs nobody and nothing to continue to exist).

Only a God like this can be truly worthy of our worship. **'For from him and through him and to him are all things. To him be the glory for ever!'**[24]

Do we need God?

'...he himself gives all men life and breath and everything else' Acts 17:25

Despite many claims to the contrary, it is becoming increasingly clear that life did not, and could not, 'just happen'. For example, these are the words of Francis Crick, famous for discovering the molecular structure of DNA. Though Crick is by no means a Christian, he wrote, 'An honest man, armed with all the knowledge available to us now, could only state that in some sense, the origin of life appears at the moment to be almost a miracle, so many are the conditions which would have had to have been satisfied to get it going.'[25] Take away the word 'almost', and the Bible is in complete agreement!

God's care for his creation is very real. He not only gives us life and breath, but he gives us enough to *maintain* life and breath. We are used to seeing whole areas—even whole countries—devastated by drought and famine. What we often forget though is that the world *always* provides enough food and water to feed all six billion of its inhabitants. God provides enough—but human greed and foolishness leave many without.

And when Paul talks about 'everything else' he is reminding us that there is more to life than we can see. We are not just animals, but spiritual beings, too—and God provides for our spiritual needs. Jesus said, **'Man does not live on bread alone, but on every word that comes from the mouth of God.'**[26]

Are humans just animals?

'...from one man he made every nation of men'
Acts 17:26

The Greeks took it for granted that they were special; everyone not born a Greek was a barbarian. Today, many people take it for granted that *no one* is special. We are 'just' animals.

For example, the ethicist, Peter Singer, has argued that now 'we know' that mankind is not a special creation of God, there are no good reasons for treating humans as special. 'If we compare a severely defective human infant with a nonhuman animal, a dog or a pig, for example, we will often find the nonhuman to have superior capacities… Species membership alone… is not morally relevant.'[27] So, he argues, we can dispense with ideas of the sanctity of human life: it has no more 'sanctity' than any other animal's life—therefore we may kill 'defective' humans with no more thought than we would give to killing a rat.

I am not convinced that many of us really believe this. We know instinctively that there is a difference between killing a rat and killing a child. We may feel outraged if we see someone drowning a sack full of unwanted kittens; but our outrage would be greater if the sack contained unwanted babies! No, we react in horror to Peter Singer's ideas, and rightly so.

But why? Singer is only being logical. The clear teaching of the Bible gives us the true justification for our horror. Humans are not *just* animals. We are the peak of God's creation. Our first parents were made directly by God and in his image.[28] Because we are descended from them, we are all made in God's image, too. Though that image is spoiled by our sin and we are, at the moment, **'a little lower than angels'**[29], we were made to rule with God.

Jesus said, **'God so loved the world that he gave his one and only Son, that whoever believes in him shall not perish but have eternal life.'**[30]

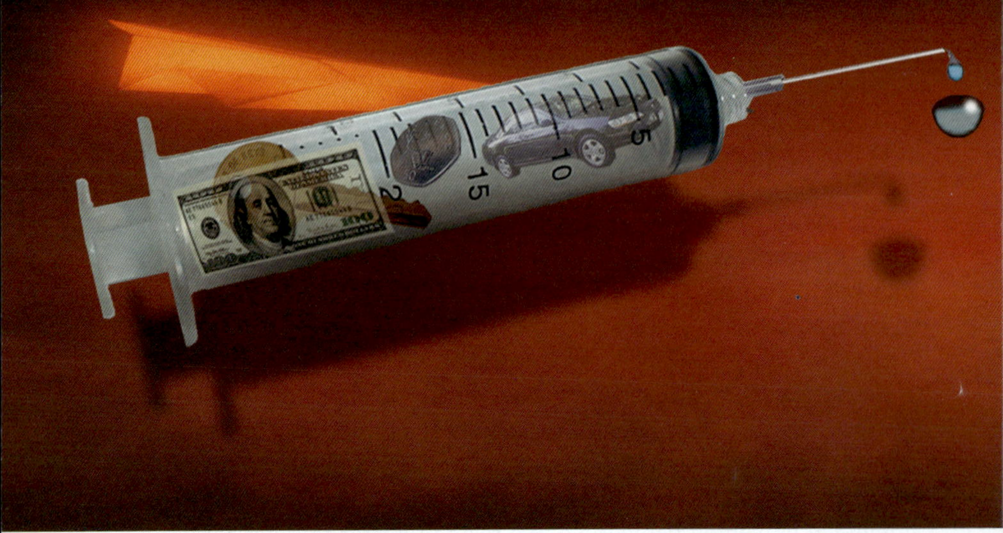

Is there a purpose?

'...he determined the times set for them... so that men would seek him and perhaps reach out for him...' Acts 17:27

In much of the world today, suicide is one of the major causes of death among young people. Although society has never been so prosperous and we have never had so many material goods, for many people life just seems pointless. It is no coincidence that this has happened at the same time as society has been losing its sense of God. Without God, and without an eternity to come, what is the point of anything?

Whatever God does, he does with a purpose. Sometimes we waste our time and effort, but God never does. The purpose for which God made human beings, says Paul, is that we might seek him, find him and have a relationship with him. Alone among all earth's creatures, we were made with the capacity to know God and find our chief joys in knowing and serving him.

This is not just a Bible idea, and Paul knows it. In verse 28, he quotes two pagan poets who were aware of this, at least dimly. But it is the Bible alone that tells us how it came to be.

Many people have tried to find satisfaction in possessions, and found only that the more they have, the more they want. It is not surprising. If we were made to be satisfied only by God, how can anything else fill that emptiness? Nothing can ever be as big as God! As Augustine said, centuries ago, 'God has made us for himself, and our hearts are restless until they find their rest in him.'

The great hymn-writer, Isaac Watts, wrote, 'Religion never was designed to make our pleasures less.'[31] He was right, for Jesus said, **'I have come that they may have life, and have it to the full,'**[32] and **'This is eternal life: that they may know you, the only true God, and Jesus Christ, whom you have sent.'**[33]

What is God like?

'...we should not think that the divine being is ... an image made by man's design' Acts 17:29

Some things about God are, says the Bible, obvious from creation itself. For '**what may be known about God is plain ... because God has made it plain... For since the creation of the world God's invisible qualities—his eternal power and divine nature—have been clearly seen, being understood from what has been made, so that men are without excuse.**'[34] Here, the Bible is saying that it is obvious from the world around us that there must *be* a God. But it is also saying that some things are also obvious *about* God. His power is one such obvious thing: to make a universe like this, God must be extraordinarily powerful. **'The heavens declare the glory of God; the skies proclaim the work of his hands.'**[35]

In spite of these obvious truths, though, the human race has often been guilty of idolatry, making images of God that fall far short of the truth they should know. (*All* images of God always fall far short of the truth!) Some people are even more extreme, and deny that there is a God at all. Why is this? Because, says the Bible, the truth makes us uncomfortable, and we **'suppress the truth by [our] wickedness'** and exchange **'the glory of the immortal God for images made to look like mortal man and birds and animals and reptiles.'**[36] We should not think like this, says Paul here in Acts 17. When we do, he says in Romans 1, it brings down God's wrath on us.[37]

Perhaps you think we are not guilty of idolatry today; it seems an old fashioned sin. Yet anything that takes the place in our life that God should have is an idol—whether it is our family, our career, money, power, relationships or anything else.

And we have no excuse. We may know exactly what God is like, for Jesus said, **'Anyone who has seen me has seen the Father.'**[38]

What does God want?

'... now he commands all people everywhere to repent ...' Acts 17:30

History has turning points: after them, things are never quite the same again. The First World War was one such turning point, destroying for ever the hope that the human race was nearing perfection! The assassination of President Kennedy was another. But the greatest turning point of them all happened two thousand years ago: it was the death of Jesus.

Before Jesus died, the human race had always been a sinful human race, and yet God had been remarkably patient. Idolatry and other sins have always abounded, crying out for judgement and punishment. Although God must always be angry with sin, he had not brought about decisive judgement: he had **'overlooked such ignorance'**.[39]

Now that things have changed, God's character and judgement are to be proclaimed throughout the world. His forgiveness is to be proclaimed, too, for Jesus died that sinners may be forgiven. But to be forgiven, we, too, need to do something: God **'commands all people everywhere to repent'**. 'Repent' means change: it is a change of mind that also changes our behaviour. We must change our mind about God, and stop leaving him out of our lives (or stop only having him on the fringes). We must change our mind about ourselves, and see that our sins are so great we can never pay for them ourselves.[42] And we must change our mind about Jesus, and realize that trusting him is our only hope. Jesus said he had come **'to give his life as a ransom for many'**.[43]

Will there be a judgement?

'... he has set a day when he will judge the world with justice by the man he has appointed...' Acts 17:31

When many people think of God, they think of a rather kindly old gentleman who could never be angry. The truth, though, is both better and worse than that!

While we know we are not perfect, we do not really think our imperfections matter very much. But the Bible calls them sin, and insists that sin is so serious that God must judge it: **'the wrath of God is being revealed from heaven against all the godlessness and wickedness of men.'**[45] Sin is serious enough to bring God's wrath.

The place where God's wrath is felt most painfully—and eternally—is hell.

It surprises many people to discover that Jesus spoke a great deal about hell. Many of the common descriptions of hell—**a place of torment,**[46] **a place of weeping and gnashing of teeth,**[47] **a place of outer darkness**[48]—actually come from Jesus himself. He knew he needed to warn us all how serious our sin is, and the imagery he uses is terrifying.

In fact, Jesus also told us that he would be the Judge: in the end, it is up to him who goes to heaven and who goes to hell.[49] Judgement is a fearsome thing, for hell is real and we have all sinned.[50] Happily, heaven is real, too—and forgiveness is possible for us all because Jesus died. Jesus said, **'This is my blood of the covenant, which is poured out for many for the forgiveness of sins.'**[51]

How can we be sure?

'...he has given proof of this to all men by raising him from the dead...' Acts 17:31

After about three years of public preaching, Jesus was arrested by the authorities and sentenced to death.[52] His claims to be God had offended them;[53] his popularity had frightened them.[54] After a sham trial in which all kinds of laws were broken by the authorities, Jesus was hastily executed by being nailed to a cross between two criminals. And that, of course, should have been the end of it. But the Bible says some surprising things about Jesus' death.

Firstly, it was *voluntary*. **'No one takes [my life] from me, but I lay it down of my own accord. I have authority to lay it down and authority to take it up again,'** *said Jesus.*[55]

Secondly, it was *for others*. **'A ransom for many'**[56] is how Jesus describes it himself. His death pays the price for our sin: **'He was pierced for our transgressions; he was crushed for our iniquities'**.[57] By Jesus' death we can be set free.

Thirdly—and most surprising of all—it was *not the end*. Three days later, Jesus rose triumphant from the dead. The Gospels declare this with one voice. It was the subject of the very first Christian sermon.[58] Paul offers it here in Acts 17 as the proof that his message is true. Everywhere in the New Testament it is taken for granted. It's a message of great joy, and gives confidence to those who believe it.

Of all the people who have ever died, only Jesus has conquered death. And just as he died for others, so he tells us that he conquered death for others: Jesus said, **'Because I live, you also will live.'**[59]

Can we prove the proof?

'...he has given proof of this to all men by raising him from the dead...' Acts 17:31

But is it true? Did Jesus rise from the dead? Can we prove the proof?

Two atheists, both lawyers, met by chance on a train and soon found themselves discussing their common atheism. As a result of the conversation, one of them, Lew Wallace, decided to spend some time researching the 'subject of religion'. As he researched his subject, he became so convinced that Jesus *had* risen from the dead that he wrote the novel *Ben Hur* (which takes the resurrection of Jesus for granted), and came to 'absolute belief in God and the Divinity of Christ'.[60]

Christianity is unique because it actually presents us with evidence that it is true. Paul knows that his hearers will have real problems with some of the ideas that he's presenting them, and he says **'[God] has given proof of this to all men by raising [Jesus] from the dead.'**

Many books have been written collecting the evidence for the resurrection together.[61] Some of the strands of evidence go something like this:

> *Jesus' tomb was empty.* The disciples could not have stolen the body, for they were willing to die rather than deny that Jesus had risen. The Roman or Jewish authorities cannot have removed the body, or they would simply have produced it when the new Christians began to be a nuisance.
>
> *The disciples changed radically*. Peter, the boldest of them all, was proved a coward when Jesus was on trial,[62] but shortly afterwards risked his own life to preach Jesus.[63]
>
> *The gospel spread rapidly*. Without any political support, or any use of force, the Christian faith spread throughout the known world in less than a generation.
>
> *There were many witnesses*—up to 500 at one time saw Jesus after he had risen.[64]

Is this evidence strong enough? A former Chief Justice of England, Lord Darling, said, 'There exists such overwhelming evidence, positive and negative, factual and circumstantial, that no intelligent jury in the world could fail to bring in a verdict that the resurrection story is true.'[65]

Jesus rose from the dead. He said, **'I lay down my life—only to take it up again.'**[66]

What about you?

'...some of them sneered... a few... believed'
Acts 17:32, 34

When Paul mentioned the resurrection of the dead, his address came to a very sudden end. It was just too much for these Greeks to accept, and they sneered. But some of his hearers were different: they wanted to hear him again, probably in more detail.

Their different reactions make the very important point: Christianity always divides people. In fact, Jesus predicted it would even divide families.[67]

Many people would see that as a good reason to pay Christianity no attention at all! But it is too important for that; what we do with Jesus and the Christian gospel is the one thing that makes the difference to where we spend eternity: **'Whoever believes in him is not condemned, but whoever does not believe stands condemned already.'**[68] Nothing could be more important.

This booklet has outlined in very short detail some of the main thrusts of the Christian gospel. Much more could be said. But at the heart of it is this simple truth: we have all sinned and placed ourselves under the judgement of an almighty, holy God. His love is so great, however, that he has sent his Son, Jesus, to bear our sins in his own body on the tree.[69] Now he commands that we turn from our sin and trust Jesus, who died for sinners. To those who do, God gives forgiveness and eternal life as a free gift.[70]

What will you do? Sneer—and be lost? Or turn, and be saved? Jesus said, **'Whoever comes to me I will never drive away.'**[71]

Turning and Trusting

'...a few... believed' Acts 17:34

If you have read this far, perhaps you are not one who sneers at the gospel of Jesus, but genuinely wants to be saved by it. What then should you do?

Let me put it as simply as I can by summarizing it in two words: *turn*, and *trust*. If you want to be a Christian, if you want to be saved, this is what you must do.

Firstly, *Turn*. There is something we must turn *from* and Someone we must turn *to*. This is what it means to be 'converted'.

We turn *from* our sin—not just our sins, but our sin. Sin is that attitude to life that leaves God out, or leaves him only at the edges. We spend our lives serving ourselves—our own wants or desires become our idols. Our sin then leads to our sins—breaking the commandments—and we must turn away from both.

We turn *to* God by calling on him to pardon and forgive us our sin for Jesus' sake. Admitting at last that there is nothing we can do to save ourselves—our debts are too big, our lives are too dirty and even our desires to change are too weak—we call on God to help us because only almighty power can make the difference we need.

Secondly, *Trust*. God has promised that **'Everyone who calls on the name of the Lord will be saved.'**[72] He has assured us that **'if we confess our sins, he is faithful and just and will forgive us our sins,'**[73] and **'the blood of Jesus, his Son, purifies us from all sin'**.[74] Jesus died for sinners, giving his life as a ransom. Faith is knowing this, believing this—and depending on it, as we try to live our lives from now on in obedience to God and fellowship with him.

If you have turned from your sin and put your trust in the Lord Jesus, it is vitally important that you begin to meet regularly with other Christians. Find a church that describes itself as 'evangelical' or 'bible-believing' and begin to go along regularly. May God bless you as you begin to grow in knowledge and in grace.

ACTS 17:16–34

16While Paul was waiting
for them in Athens, he was
greatly distressed to see
that the city was full of idols.
17So he reasoned in the
synagogue with the Jews
and the God-fearing
Greeks, as well as in the
marketplace day by day
with those who happened to
be there. 18A group of
Epicurean and Stoic
philosophers began to
dispute with him. Some of
them asked, "What is this
babbler trying to say?"
Others remarked, "He
seems to be advocating
foreign gods." They said this
because Paul was
preaching the good news
about Jesus and the
resurrection. 19Then they
took him and brought him to
a meeting of the Areopagus,
where they said to him,
"May we know what this
new teaching is that you are
presenting? 20You are
bringing some strange
ideas to our ears, and we
want to know what they
mean." 21(All the Athenians
and the foreigners who lived
there spent their time doing
nothing but talking about
and listening to the latest
ideas.)
22Paul then stood up in
the meeting of the
Areopagus and said: "Men
of Athens! I see that in
every way you are very
religious. 23For as I walked
around and looked carefully
at your objects of worship, I
even found an altar with this
inscription: TO AN
UNKNOWN GOD. Now
what you worship as
something unknown I am
going to proclaim to you.
24"The God who made
the world and everything in
it is the Lord of heaven and
earth and does not live in
temples built by hands.
25And he is not served by
human hands, as if he
needed anything, because
he himself gives all men life
and breath and everything
else. 26From one man he
made every nation of men,
that they should inhabit the
whole earth; and he
determined the times set for
them and the exact places
where they should live.
27God did this so that men
would seek him and
perhaps reach out for him
and find him, though he is
not far from each one of us.
28'For in him we live and
move and have our being.'
As some of your own poets
have said, 'We are his
offspring.'
29"Therefore since we are
God's offspring, we should
not think that the divine
being is like gold or silver or
stone—an image made by
man's design and skill. 30In
the past God overlooked
such ignorance, but now he
commands all people
everywhere to repent.
31For he has set a day
when he will judge the
world with justice by the
man he has appointed. He
has given proof of this to all
men by raising him from the
dead."
32When they heard about
the resurrection of the
dead, some of them
sneered, but others said,
"We want to hear you again
on this subject." 33At that,
Paul left the Council. 34A
few men became followers
of Paul and believed.
Among them was
Dionysius, a member of the
Areopagus, also a woman
named Damaris, and a
number of others.